Trust

Sue Leather and Julian Thomlinson

T0349311

Series Editor: Rob Waring
Story Editor: Julian Thomlinson
Series Development Editor: Sue Leather

HEINLE
CENGAGE Learning

Australia • Brazil • Japan • Korea • Mexico • Singapore • Spain • United Kingdom • United States

HEINLE
CENGAGE Learning™

Page Turners Reading Library

Trust
Sue Leather and Julian Thomlinson

Publisher: Andrew Robinson

Executive Editor: Sean Bermingham

Senior Development Editor:
Derek Mackrell

Assistant Editor: Sarah Tan

Director of Global Marketing:
Ian Martin

Content Project Manager:
Tan Jin Hock

Print Buyer:
Susan Spencer

Layout Design and Illustrations:
Redbean Design Pte Ltd

Cover Illustration: Eric Foenander

Photo Credits:
45 (from top to bottom)
dslaven/Shutterstock, artproem/
Shutterstock, Wikimedia Commons

ISBN-13: 978-1-4240-4644-7

ISBN-10: 1-4240-4644-0

Heinle
20 Channel Center Street
Boston, Massachusetts 02210
USA

Cengage Learning is a leading provider of customized learning solutions with office locations around the globe, including Singapore, the United Kingdom, Australia, Mexico, Brazil, and Japan. Locate your local office at:
international.cengage.com/region

Cengage Learning products are represented in Canada by Nelson Education, Ltd.

Visit Heinle online at **elt.heinle.com**

Visit our corporate website at
www.cengage.com

Printed in the United States of America
1 2 3 4 5 6 7 – 14 13 12 11 10

Contents

Background Reading

People in the story

Sandra Marks
Sandra is a communications
student and editor of
The Brenton Sun
online newspaper.

Felipe Rosas
Felipe is also a
communications student
and a reporter for
The Brenton Sun
online newspaper.

Robert Marks
Robert is Sandra's father. He
is head of State Realty and a
member of the Brenton College
Board of Governors.

Professor Melanie Saunders
Professor Saunders is head
of Media Studies at Brenton
College. She helps students
with their problems.

This story is set in Brenton, a college town in the
northwestern United States.

Chapter 1

Problems here, problems there

It was her first day as editor of the college online newspaper, *The Brenton Sun,* and Sandra had a thousand things to do. The phone had been ringing all morning, and she hadn't eaten breakfast. It was now almost eleven o'clock, and she had three stories to finish before lunch.

I just need some time, she thought, *some quiet time, so I can finish these stories.* There was a knock at the door. *I hope it's not Felipe.*

"Come in," she said, quietly, and Felipe walked in.

Today, it seemed, was one of those days.

Just a few months ago, Sandra and Felipe had been friends. Good friends. But *The Brenton Sun* had needed an editor, and Sandra and Felipe both wanted the job. Sandra got it, and she knew Felipe wasn't happy about it. No, Felipe wasn't happy about it at all. This was going to be the first time they spoke since the summer. And it wasn't going to be easy.

Sandra hoped things could be the same between Felipe and her. She hoped they could be friends, just like they were before. *I need to be nice about this,* Sandra thought to herself. *It's a difficult situation and I need to be nice.*

"Hi, Felipe," Sandra said.

"Hey, *boss*," Felipe replied.

"How was your summer?" Sandra began.

"Summer was fine, thanks. So, have you got anything for me?"

Sandra could see that Felipe didn't want to just talk. Maybe it wasn't going to be easy to be nice.

"Let's see," she began. "We need a story on the movie festival next month."

"No, I don't think so," replied Felipe. "Give that to Jenny or Symon."

"What about this? Vice President De Veer wants a story about the new Fairway Hotel and Golf Course opening on Wednesday?"

She put a piece of paper on the desk.

"The information's all here . . ."

"It sounds a little boring, Sandra. Don't you have anything better?"

Felipe, Sandra knew, was probably the best reporter in the college. But she knew the reason he didn't get the editor's job was because he was difficult. And now he was being difficult with her.

"Listen, Felipe, I'm sorry it's boring. But these are the stories I need. I've got a busy day and I need you to help me."

Sandra didn't like the way her voice sounded. It sounded weak. *Who's the boss now?* she asked herself.

"Why don't you do the Fairway story yourself? Your father will be there, won't he?" Felipe said.

"Yes, he'll be there. So what?"

Felipe smiled at her. Sandra didn't like the smile. Sandra's father, Robert Marks, was head of Washington State Realty. His job was to give permission for all the big land sales and developments in the city. That made him a powerful man around the city. He was also on the Board of Governors at Brenton College. Some people thought that Sandra was the new editor of *The Brenton Sun* because of her father. Sandra knew it wasn't true because she knew her father. Robert Marks was the most loving father in the world. He would do anything for his daughter, but he wouldn't tell lies. When she got the job, she had asked him, "Did you help me?" And her father had said "No," so that was that. No, it wasn't true, but some people thought it was. *And now Felipe thinks it,* she thought to herself. It hurt, because they were once good friends. *More than friends* . . . She could feel herself getting upset.

"Please, Felipe. Will you please do one of these stories?"

Felipe smiled. Somehow that made it even worse, Sandra thought.

"Sure, boss," he said. He picked up the paper from her desk and left the room without looking at her.

◇◇◇

It was ten o'clock in the evening by the time Sandra arrived home. As she let herself into the house, her dog, Walt, came to the door to greet her. As she bent down to pet her dog, she heard her father talking in the living room. *Ken must be here,* Sandra thought.

Ken Bains was her father's best friend. They had been friends since school and now they worked together for the Washington State Realty Commission. Ken was like an uncle to Sandra. Sandra liked Ken because he could always make her laugh, but more than that, she liked him because he was always a friend to her dad, even in the worst of times. When Sandra's mother, Grace, died a few years ago, Robert had been really sad. And Ken Bains helped him.

"Here she is!" said Ken, with his big smile.

"I'm happy you're home, darling," her father said, standing and kissing her cheek. "I was a little worried about you."

"Sorry I'm late, Daddy. I was really busy today. Nice to see you, Ken."

"And you," Ken said. He kissed her cheek.

"Ken brought some food for us," her father went on. "You can sit and eat and tell me all about your first day as editor."

"What kind?" Sandra asked.

"Chinese, of course!" Ken said. It was Sandra's favorite, and Ken always brought it. Sandra took it from Ken and put it on the table.

"I have to go," said Ken. "It's late, and I'm sure you two want to talk."

"Oh, don't go!" Sandra said.

"Are you sure, Ken?"

"I really have to," Ken said. "This old man needs his rest."

"Hey! I'm older than you," said Robert, and the two men laughed as they walked to the door.

While Sandra ate, her father stood with Ken at the door. They talked in low voices for a moment, then Robert came back in and sat with her. "You must be tired, Sandy. How was your day?" Her father always called her "Sandy."

Between mouthfuls, she told him about the stories she wrote, and all the phone calls, and not eating anything until three o'clock. She tried not to think about Felipe.

"What about you, Daddy? Did you have a nice time with Ken?"

"Oh, we were just finishing off some work."

Sandra thought he looked tired, suddenly.

"Hey, Daddy, is everything all right?" she asked.

"Sure. Why?" he replied.

"You just seem so . . . I don't know . . . quiet."

Now she thought about it, Sandra realized her father was quiet a lot these days.

"It's nothing. Just some things at work."

"What's wrong?"

"Oh, the usual, I suppose. Problems here, problems there. I'm sure you can understand that." He smiled at her.

"Yeah, I can," Sandra replied.

"Hey, what about Felipe?" her father asked. "Was he OK about you being editor?"

"Well, not really. But I'm sure it'll be fine," she said. She wasn't sure, but she didn't want to make her father worry.

"Good girl. It's always going to be difficult at first. It was like that with me and Ken when I got the job he wanted too. It'll be all right. Felipe's a good kid, Sandy. I think you can trust him. You know, I miss seeing him myself."

"Oh, you'll see him on Wednesday. He's doing the Fairway opening story for the paper."

"Oh, good, good," her father said. He seemed far away again, as if he wasn't really there.

"Daddy, are you sure you're all right?"

"I'm sure, I'm sure. Really, Sandy, it's nothing," he said.

Chapter 2

Felipe's story

Sandra came into *The Brenton Sun* office on Thursday morning to find Felipe already there, working at his computer. He had his back to her and didn't hear her come in. As she walked by, Sandra saw a picture of her father on his computer screen. It looked like a news article. This was strange, she thought. The story about the Fairway opening was already finished. Why was he looking at a story about her father now? She walked over to him to ask.

"Felipe . . ."

Felipe turned around quickly, his eyes wide.

"Sandra, hi . . ." He turned back to his computer and suddenly closed the screen. "I didn't see you there. Good morning. How are you?"

"Felipe, why are you looking at a story about my father? You finished the Fairway story yesterday."

"Oh, no, it was nothing," Felipe replied. "It was just the news. I was just reading the news."

"So why did you close it when you saw me?"

"Oh, you know. I don't know, really," Felipe said. "Anyway, how are you?"

"Felipe, could I see that story, please?" Sandra asked.

"Now? I mean, I can send you the link to the website if . . ."

"Yes. Now, please."

Felipe opened the web page. It was a story about her father from two years ago, about the opening of the Grosvenor Hotel in Seattle. In the photo, he was standing with another man at the front of the hotel. They were both smiling.

"What is this, Felipe?" Sandra asked.

"Oh, I was just looking through some of your father's other developments. You know, after seeing him at the Fairway Golf Course yesterday."

"I can see that," Sandra said. "But why?"

"I was just trying to remember the name of this hotel. I couldn't remember it, you see. That was all."

"Oh. OK. Well, let me get a coffee and then let's go over today's stories."

"OK, sure, Sandra."

Sandra went into her office and put on some coffee. Something wasn't right. Felipe had told her he was reading the news. Why was he lying? Why was he reading about her father?

Sandra wanted to ask Felipe again later, but as the day went on she got very busy with her studies and *The Brenton Sun* and she forgot all about it.

Soon it was the weekend. Sandra always spent Sundays with her father. Usually they went to the mountains or the sea, or if the weather was bad, they went to the movies. But this weekend, they were both just too busy—she had to go into college to finish some coursework, and her father was playing golf with some business friends.

"I'm really sorry, Sandy," he told her. "I forgot all about it."

"Daddy, don't worry about me. I've got things to do, too," Sandra said. "How about dinner later?"

"I'm going to be late, Sandy. What about tomorrow? We can go to Jojo's."

"Sure thing, Daddy."

She kissed him and drove down to Brenton. She wanted to go to the library, but decided to go to *The Brenton Sun* office first, to pick up some books. As she got to the door, she heard some people talking inside. That was strange. It was Sunday and it was usually closed—she even had her keys with her. She decided to listen and see who it was, so she put her ear to the door. She heard Jenny's voice.

"You can't do that, Felipe," Jenny said. "You have to tell Sandra first, I mean, it's her father. You have to tell her."

What's going on here? Sandra thought.

Then she heard Symon's voice.

"I agree with Jenny. I don't think we can put this on the website."

The website? They must be talking about *The Brenton Sun.* Sandra listened carefully.

"I think we need to give it to the police," Symon said.

The police?!

"Maybe you're right," Felipe said. "But it's clear enough though: Robert Marks is taking money from developers."

What?! Sandra realized her heart almost stopped for a moment. She couldn't breathe. *Daddy? Taking money from developers?* Sandra knew that developers sometimes tried to give money or gifts to people like her father, to get good contracts. But she knew her father didn't do this, would never do this.

She was angry—really angry. Sandra knew Felipe wasn't happy with her as the editor, as his boss. But to do something like this, behind her back! And to talk to Jenny and Symon about it! Felipe was trying to say bad things about her father because he wasn't happy with her.

I knew he was doing something strange, she thought. *I knew when I saw him looking at those pictures. But this stops right now.*

She opened the office door and walked into the room.

Chapter 3

The numbers never lie

"Sandra!" Felipe said. Jenny and Symon stood and looked at her, their mouths open. "What is going on here?" Sandra asked. "And before you say anything, I heard everything."

Felipe didn't speak for a moment.

"I'm sorry, Sandra," said Felipe carefully. "Really, I am. The thing is . . . there seems to be proof that your dad is taking money—bribes—from developers for giving them projects."

"Proof? What proof?" Sandra moved closer to Felipe. She had an angry look on her face.

"Take it easy," Felipe said. He led her to his computer and turned it on.

"Look," he said. He opened something on the computer desktop, a document called MARKS.

The document was a list of bids for building contracts over the last six years.

"The winning bids are here, in this column," Felipe said. "This is the Fairway contract."

Sandra looked. Hal Maxwell's name was by the bid. He was a well-known developer in the state. His name appeared many times in the document, almost always as the winner of bids.

"In the other columns are the losing bids," Felipe went on. Sandra saw that the numbers were higher than the winners: the lowest bidder always won because the government wanted the least expensive companies.

"Do you see anything strange?" Felipe asked.

It did seem strange that Hal Maxwell won almost all of his bids. But she knew Hal Maxwell had a good reputation. Her father said that he was cheap and did good work.

"If you're talking about Hal Maxwell winning most of his bids, then there's nothing strange about that. Daddy's told me about him before: he's cheap and he's good at his job. Daddy knows him well."

Felipe smiled.

"You said that, not me, Sandra," he said. "But that's not what I'm talking about, not really."

"You need to look at how much the bids win by," Symon said. Symon was a math student.

"What do you mean?" Sandra asked.

"See here." Symon put his finger on a bid from two years ago. The winner was a developer named John Rowe.

"Rowe's bid was $170,000 less than the next bid. It's a big difference."

Symon showed Sandra other examples, all with a big difference between the winner's bids and the losers' bids.

"Now look at Maxwell's bids," Symon said.

Sandra looked. Almost all of Maxwell's winning bids were only a few thousand dollars under the prices of the other bidders. *It's almost as if Maxwell knows what is happening!* Sandra thought. *Maybe someone's telling him?* This was strange, she knew. Sometimes a developer could be lucky, to win a bid by only a small difference. But every time?

Nobody spoke as Sandra studied the document in front of her. She looked at it again and again, trying to find a reason. The more she studied it, the worse it looked. It wasn't just Maxwell either. There were two other developers winning with very strange bids: Jim Malone and Gina LaHoya.

"You know what this means, don't you?" Felipe asked.

Sandra knew. It meant that someone was telling Maxwell how much to bid. Someone who knew everyone else's bids so they could win the contract. Someone like her father.

Suddenly Sandra needed to sit down.

"Maxwell knew how much to bid, Sandra. He knew. The only people with that information were . . ."

"In my father's office, I know," Sandra said. "But Daddy . . . I just don't believe it."

"I didn't believe it either," said Felipe. "You know how much I like your father. But the numbers never lie, Sandra."

"Where did this information come from?" Sandra asked.

"I heard John Rowe talking at the Fairway opening," Felipe said. "He was angry at losing to Maxwell by $2,000. He said it was the third time."

"Maybe he's just angry because he didn't win," Sandra said. "Maybe he's . . ."

"Maybe so, but it made me think. I read about something like this happening in Florida a few years ago."

"So I called the other developers, asking them for their bids on other contracts," Symon said quickly. "I said it was for a math project."

"And we put the information together from there," Felipe said.

"And you were going to go to the police without telling me?" Sandra asked.

Felipe didn't reply for a moment.

"He's your father, Sandra."

"We didn't know what to do," Jenny said. She looked unhappy about it all. "That's why we were talking."

"You can see how bad it looks though, can't you?" Felipe asked her.

She could see all right. As Felipe said, the numbers never lie. *But neither does my father,* she thought.

"Give me some time," she asked. "I'll talk to my father and get the truth about this."

"Sandra . . ." Felipe began.

"24 hours. That's all. Please, Felipe."

Felipe looked at Jenny and Symon. They both nodded their heads.

"OK," he said. "24 hours."

Chapter 4

24 hours

Sandra left the office and phoned her father. She didn't know what to say to him but she knew she had to say something. But he didn't answer. She tried again, but there was still no answer. Sandra threw the phone back in her bag and sat down on a nearby wall. This was strange—he always had the answering machine on. *His phone must be switched off,* she thought. *But why?*

Sandra started to worry about it, then stopped herself. *Wait a second, girl,* she thought. *So he's switched his phone off. It doesn't mean he's taking money from developers.*

He's driving or playing golf already, she thought. Where was the game again? Did her father tell her? She couldn't remember. Ken would know. She took her phone out and tried Ken's number. But he didn't answer either. *Maybe if I go home I can check his diary or something,* she thought, *find out where he's playing golf.* She drove back thinking about what to say. She just didn't know. It made her crazy. *It's my job to think of the right words,* she thought. *So why can't I think of them now?*

When she got home she went straight upstairs to her father's office. It felt strange to be in there without him. Her father was a lovely, kind man, but he didn't like her going in his office, she knew.

"Everyone needs a place nobody else can go," he once told her. "Mine is my office."

She never thought there was anything strange about this before.

Now she wasn't so sure.

Still, she felt bad going in there, and though she knew he was out, she kept looking over her shoulder, as if he was about to come in.

His phone was sitting on the desk next to his computer. *At least I know why he didn't answer,* Sandra thought. She looked for his diary. He usually kept it in the desk drawer, but it was locked. He carried the key around with him, she knew. *I guess that's that, then,* she thought, then looked at the computer.

Maybe there'll be an e-mail about the golf game, she thought. *But am I really going to look at my daddy's e-mail?*

She decided she was, and turned the computer on. It was old, and the computer virus software took time to start up. *Come on, hurry up, computer!* she thought. After a few minutes it asked her for a password.

First she tried "Mariners," her dad's favorite baseball team. Wrong. Then she tried her name, then her birthday, then her name and her birthday. Wrong, wrong, and wrong. *What could it be?* she thought. *It must be something he could never forget.*

She typed "G-R-A-C-E-0-4-1-4."

Her mother's name and birthday.

She was in.

Sandra opened her father's e-mail and looked for "golf." Nothing, at least nothing about today's game. She told herself she was only looking for information about the golf game, but she also knew that if her father was taking bribes, there would probably be some information about it on the computer.

I can't, she thought to herself. *I can't go behind his back like this. Looking at his personal stuff . . .*

You have to do something, said a voice in her mind.

She began to look through his other e-mails, first searching for information about the Fairway, then the other contracts on the list. There were many e-mails about the contracts, but nothing strange.

Where else can I look? she thought. She closed the e-mail and opened the "work" folder . . .

Suddenly there was a noise outside the door. Sandra's heart jumped into her throat. Was her father home? She sat, helplessly, as the door slowly opened . . . and Walt walked into the room and lay down on the floor.

"You scared the life out of me, you silly dog!" she said. "Just stay there and keep quiet."

Walt closed his eyes, and Sandra went back to the computer. She looked through the work folder, reading document after document, but didn't find anything. She looked at her watch. It was two o'clock. *I can't do much more here,* she thought, and turned off the computer.

She was happy that she couldn't find anything, but she was still worried. *What can I do now?* she asked herself. She decided to make some coffee, but as she got up she knocked her pen off the desk. She bent down to get it and saw a black box on the floor, just under the desk. *A hard drive.* She'd never seen it before, but it seemed to be connected to the computer. *What do we have here?*

She found the switch on the back of the drive and turned the computer back on. There were two folders on the hard drive: "bids" and "accounts." Sandra opened the bids folder and found documents named after building contracts. The last one was for the Fairway Hotel. This was it. This was what she was looking for. She opened it, her heart beating fast.

Before she could read it, she heard another noise, and Walt started barking downstairs. *I didn't even know he'd gone,* she thought. *He must want something to eat. Well,*

he'll have to wait. She went back to the Fairway document and began to read. It started with the bids for the contract, the same as the ones on the document Felipe had showed her. She wanted to read more, but she couldn't, because there was another noise on the stairs, and too late she realized that this wasn't Walt at all, this was a person, and the person was coming into the room.

"Hi, Daddy," Sandra said.

Chapter 5

Trust

"I can't believe you didn't trust me, Sandy, I just can't believe it."

Sandra and her father sat in the living room downstairs, looking at each other. After he had found her in his office, Sandra had told him everything: about what Felipe had said, about wanting to go to the police, about her trying to talk to him, and then thinking she could just check for herself . . .

"Daddy, I did trust you! I just thought that I could . . . you know, if I looked and didn't find anything, then . . . I don't know."

Robert Marks didn't seem to care that Felipe believed he was taking money from developers. He didn't seem to care that there was talk of contacting the police, or writing the story. All he cared about was that his daughter didn't trust him.

"Daddy, I just looked to find out where you were playing golf. I never believed what Felipe said. Never! But he showed me the information, about the bids, and I didn't know what to think. You seemed really tired lately, and you've been having trouble at work . . ."

"So you thought that meant I was taking bribes?"

"I was trying to help," she said quietly. "Why did you come back anyway?"

"I forgot my phone," her father said. He stood up and looked out of the window—he seemed to be thinking.

"We know there's a problem, of course," he said. "The files you found, the pattern you saw—it's clear to us as well. Hal Maxwell, Jim Malone, and Gina LaHoya— these three always seem to know just how much to bid. They must be getting this information from somewhere. But it's not from us, and it's driving us crazy."

"When you say 'us,' you mean . . ."

"Me and Ken. We're the only ones who have the information. You see, a company who wants the project doesn't want the other companies to know their price or they will bid just below their price and win the project. So to keep the prices secret, the companies have to put their price in a secret file on our website. They give Ken and me one password each but we can only open them after the bidding finishes. I can't know the bidding prices before the bidding stops, because I don't know Ken's password and he doesn't know mine. So . . ."

"I see," Sandra said. "Daddy, I know it's not you, but you don't think it could be . . ."

"Ken?" her father asked. "How could you say that?"

"I know, Daddy, but who else could it be?" asked Sandra. "Could he break into the computer system somehow before the bids close and find out the other companies' prices, and then tell Maxwell?"

Her father went quiet and sounded very tired when he spoke again.

"I've thought about it, too. I mean, I know it's not me. But Ken can't know the prices until the files are opened, and he needs two passwords to open them."

Sandra thought about this. Then she asked, "Daddy, do you still have some documents from old projects on your computer?"

"Why?"

"Well, I'd like to see how the bidding system works. Maybe I can help."

Her father opened an old project on his computer. "This is one we did recently," he said. "I don't need Ken's password because the bidding date passed last week."

The document started to open. Then suddenly something came on the screen.

"Huh? What's this?" he asked.

"Daddy, it's a warning message about a computer virus. You have a virus on your computer. It's called *B72kTrojan*. There, can you see?"

"Yes, but how did I get it? It didn't have this virus when I opened it last week on the office computer, and I haven't opened it since then."

"Does your office computer have virus software?" she asked.

"Umm, no, it slows down the computer, so I don't use it."

"Hmm," she said, thinking. "So that means the virus was there last week. Can you ask the computer people at your office to check where the virus came from and when? Then maybe they can find out who has been playing with the files."

"Great idea!" He called the computer people at his company and asked them for the information.

A few minutes later, the computer people called back. Her father picked up the phone. "Oh, I see," he said. His face looked gray. "Are you sure? Really sure? Two weeks ago. Okay, thank you." He put down the phone.

"That was the computer people," he said. "They scanned the office computers to find where the virus came from. They found the virus on Ken's computer. And only on Ken's computer . . . The document got the virus a week *before* the bidding closed . . ."

"So Ken found a way to open the documents before the bidding finished . . ." Sandra said. She stopped and looked at her father.

Her father sat with his head in his hands. His body was shaking. When he looked up to speak, she could see he was crying.

"He was like a brother to me, Sandy. I trusted him . . . I trusted him with my life."

"Oh, Daddy, I'm so sorry."

Sandra thought about how Ken had always been there for her father when her mother died. He really helped her father over the years. She put her arms around her father and held him. He seemed very old suddenly.

"I trusted him, Sandy," he kept saying. "I trusted him."

Chapter 6

The new editor

Sandra took a few days off to be with her father and didn't go back to college until the following Wednesday. The story of her father's friend and partner taking money from developers was big news by then. After Sandra and her father found out about Ken taking money, her father drove back to the golf course to talk to him. Sandra didn't know what he said, but she did know that right after, he called the police and showed them what he and Sandra had found. The police went to arrest Ken, but Ken ran away. The story was all over the news, and the police picked Ken up two days later when he tried to go into Canada with a bag of money. The police also picked up Hal Maxwell and the other developers, and news reporters were outside Sandra's house every day, wanting to speak to her father.

It was all over the news, but not *The Brenton Sun*. When her father went to speak to Ken, Sandra called Professor Saunders and explained the situation. She asked if she could take a few days off. Sure, Professor Saunders had said. Felipe and the others called her every day, but she didn't speak to them. Not until now.

Everyone was in *The Brenton Sun* office when she arrived: Felipe, Symon, Jenny, everyone. She expected that. She had sent them a text the night before saying she was coming in. Still, they looked surprised when she walked in.

"Morning, everyone," Sandra said, taking a coffee from the machine. "Felipe, I'd like to speak to you in about ten minutes."

"Sure, Sandra," he said.

"Sandra, are you OK?" Jenny asked her.

"I'm fine," Sandra replied.

She went into her office and sat down. She knew it would be hard, coming back in. She was so angry with everyone for going behind her back. But she also knew that they were just trying to do their job. But Felipe . . . she had to deal with Felipe. She had to know if Felipe was going to make more trouble for her. And if he was? Well, one of them had to go.

She read her e-mail messages as she waited for him to arrive. Ten minutes later he knocked at the door and came in.

"Sandra, listen," he began.

"No, Felipe, you listen to me," she said. "I want us to be clear about what happened. You find a story, and you think it involves my father. You don't come to me, either as editor or friend, about it. But you work on the story behind my back, and discuss whether to put it on the college website or go to the police."

"Sandra, please," Felipe said.

"Let me finish. You do this, and I think you do it because you don't like me being the editor. You do it because you think my father got me this job, and you're angry with him and me. Is that right, Felipe?"

"Sandra, this wasn't about you being the editor. I found a story and I followed it."

"But you were wrong, Felipe, weren't you? You followed the story and you got it wrong! I trusted you, Felipe. My father trusted you."

Felipe went quiet for a moment. Sandra knew she had to be very careful with the rest of it.

"I spoke to Professor Saunders," Sandra said, "about what happened. She told me that if I don't want you on the team, you're off."

"I know that I made a mistake," Felipe said. "I know that. It's true: I wasn't happy with you as editor. I thought I was a better choice. I see I was wrong about that."

"Felipe, I can't work with someone I can't trust."

"I know that. So do the others," Felipe said. "But give me a chance. You know how much I want to be a reporter. You know, don't you?"

"Felipe, you have to promise me. You have to promise me never to do anything like this again."

"I promise."

"OK. Let's see how it goes. Anyway, I've got four stories here. Do you want any of them?"

"I'll do whatever you want me to do," he said.

"OK," Sandra replied. "You can do all four. I need you to finish them by two o'clock."

Felipe looked shocked and hurt.

"Really?" he asked.

"It was a joke," Sandra said. Felipe tried to laugh, and picked up the story on top.

"Thanks, Sandra," he said. "Thanks a lot."

Sandra watched him close the door as he left her office. Things were going to be different now between them, she could see that. *It's always different,* she said to herself, *even if you don't want it to be.*

Sandra looked at her e-mails. There were hundreds of them waiting for her reply. She took a drink of her coffee and began to read.

Review

A. Match the characters in the story to their descriptions.

1. _____ Sandra Marks   **a.** a reporter for *The Brenton Sun*
2. _____ Felipe Rosas   **b.** the head of Washington State Realty
3. _____ Robert Marks   **c.** a friend of the Marks family
4. _____ Hal Maxwell   **d.** the editor of *The Brenton Sun*
5. _____ Ken Bains   **e.** a well-known developer

B. Choose the best answer for each question.

1. How does Sandra find out that Felipe is investigating a case on her father?
   a. She hears about it from Jenny and Symon.
   b. She overhears him talking about it to Jenny and Symon.
   c. She overhears him talking to the police.
   d. She catches him writing the story on his computer.

2. How does Sandra's father feel after finding her in his office?
   a. He is hurt that she does not trust him.
   b. He is angry that she went into his office.
   c. He is scared that she has discovered all his secrets.
   d. He is surprised that she accused his best friend Ken.

3. Felipe thinks Robert Marks is _____.
   a. stealing from the Washington State Realty
   b. stealing from the developers
   c. telling developers how much to bid
   d. covering up for Ken Bains

4. In the end, what was Felipe's reason for going behind Sandra's back?
   a. He wanted to show he was a good reporter.
   b. He did not like Sandra being his boss.
   c. He did not like Sandra or her father.
   d. He was worried about how Sandra would react.

C. Read each statement and circle whether it is true (T) or false (F).

1. Sandra has been the editor of *The Brenton Sun* for a year. **T / F**
2. Felipe is a better reporter than Sandra. **T / F**
3. The developer with the highest bid usually wins the contract. **T / F**
4. Robert Marks uses his daughter's name as his computer password. **T / F**
5. Robert and Ken have been best friends since school. **T / F**
6. Ken agrees to give himself up to the police. **T / F**
7. In the end, Sandra and Felipe are good friends again. **T / F**

D. Complete each sentence with the correct word from the box.

bribe	editor	virus	proof
trust	contract	permission	reporter

1. A(n) _____ is an agreement to sell or do something at an agreed price.
2. A(n) _____ is a file or program which can harm your computer.
3. A(n) _____ is the person in charge of a newspaper or magazine.
4. A(n) _____ is a secret payment made to someone to influence his decision.
5. To have _____ of something is to have facts to show it is true.
6. If you _____ someone, you believe in that person.
7. If you have _____ to do something, you are allowed to do it.
8. A(n) _____ is someone who finds and writes news stories.

Background Reading:

Spotlight on ... *Auctions*

An auction is a special sale where items are sold to the person who pays the highest price. In traditional auctions, people sit in a room and bid for items by calling out the price. Nowadays, auctions are done online, on websites like eBay.

How much do you think people are willing to pay for things they *really* want? Here are some of the most expensive items ever sold at auctions.

Item	Year Sold	Price
A piece of Elvis Presley's hair	2002	$115,000
Marilyn Monroe's *"Happy Birthday Mr. President"* dress	1999	$1,267,500
Mark McGwire's (a famous baseball player) 70th-home-run baseball	1999	$3,000,000
Guarneri del Gesù violin	2007	$3,900,000
1957 *Ferrari 250 Testa Rossa*	2009	$12,200,000
Wittelsbach diamond	2008	$23,400,000
Roman-era statue, *Artemis and the Stag*	2007	$28,600,000
Leonardo Da Vinci's *Codex Hammer*	1984	$30,802,500
Badminton Cabinet	2004	$36,000,000
Pablo Picasso's *Boy with a Pipe*	2004	$104,100,000

Think About It

1. If you were very rich, what would you buy at an auction?

2. Have you ever purchased anything at an online auction? What did you buy?

Glossary

bid	(*n., v.*)	If a company bids for a contract, it states the price it will do the work for.
bribe	(*n., v.*)	If you accept a bribe, you get money secretly when you shouldn't.
contract	(*n.*)	A business contract is an agreement to sell or do something at a certain price.
developer	(*n.*)	A developer is a person or a company that builds things.
document	(*n.*)	A computer document is a file such as a letter that you can read on a computer.
partner	(*n.*)	Your partner is someone you work with in business.
password	(*n.*)	A password is a secret word you use to get access to a computer or banking information.
permission/permit	(*n.*)	When you get permission or a permit to do something, you are then allowed to do it.
professional	(*n.*)	A professional is someone who is qualified for the job, such as a teacher, lawyer, or doctor.
promise	(*n., v.*)	When you make a promise, you say that you will do something.
project	(*n.*)	In business, a project is a piece of work, such as designing a building.
proof	(*n.*)	When you have proof that someone did something wrong, then you have evidence that they did it.
realty	(*adj.*)	A realty company helps people buy and sell land and buildings.
reporter	(*n.*)	A reporter is a person who writes news stories for a newspaper.
screen	(*n.*)	A computer screen is the part of the computer where you can see files and documents.
shocked	(*adj.*)	If you are shocked by something, you are unpleasantly surprised.
trust	(*n., v.*)	If you trust someone, you believe in him or her.
virus	(*n., v.*)	A computer virus is a file that can damage your computer.